EARTH LINES

POEMS FOR THE GREEN AGE

by PAT MOON

Greenwillow Books, New York

Copyright © 1991 by Pat Moon
First published in Great Britain in 1991 by Pimlico Publishing Ltd.
Revised edition published in the United States in 1993 by Greenwillow Books.
Printed in the United States of America
First American Edition   10 9 8 7 6 5 4 3 2 1

Interior text design of original edition by Bob Hall

▲▲

Library of Congress Cataloging-in-Publication Data
Moon, Pat.
Earth lines : poems for the green age / by Pat Moon.
p. cm.
Summary: The author's poems celebrate Earth and reflect
a concern for its survival in an age of pollution.
ISBN 0-688-11853-4
1. Nature—Juvenile poetry.
2. Ecology—Juvenile poetry.
3. Environmental protection—Juvenile poetry.
4. Children's poetry, English.
[1. Nature—Poetry. 2. Pollution—Poetry.
3. Environmental protection—Poetry.
4. English poetry.]   I. Title.
PR6063.05825E24   1993
821'.914—dc20
92-27570 CIP   AC

▲▲▲▲▲▲▲▲▲▲▲▲▲▲▲▲▲▲▲▲▲▲▲▲▲▲▲▲▲▲▲▲

This book
is dedicated to
David, Daisy, Sam and Ben

$\mathcal{T}$his book began when I was asked if I would be interested in writing a collection of poems that not only celebrated our planet Earth, but also reflected the concern we all feel for its healthy survival.

You will see that many of them ask questions, for I believe that this is what the Green Age is all about: a time when we are beginning to question our lifestyles that use up so much of the earth's riches but put so little back, except in the form of waste and pollution. There are poems that express a sense of wonder for our world and some lighter verses too, for I think humour is not only vital in keeping a sense of balance but can also be an effective way of conveying a message.

It is an age when we are realising that everything we do has a consequence. How many of us would have thought a decade ago that our taste for hamburgers would threaten the rainforests, or that aerosol cans could damage the ozone layer?

There is a growing awareness of the effect our lifestyle has on the poorer peoples of the Third World and their environment as well as the widening gap between rich and poor, old and young, privileged and deprived in the wealthier countries too. We are rediscovering the truth that we must look after all the things that look after us. The forests, the seas and the air we breathe, our animal life, our family and community.

It is often true that we do not value what we have until we have lost it. We can no longer choose to ignore the warning signs, for if we do not change our ways the quality of our lives will suffer. For a safe, friendly, healthy environment each one of us can and must contribute before it is too late.

Writing this book has made me revalue this wonderful world, to ask questions and to make changes in the way I live. I hope it prompts you to ask questions too, for only by asking questions shall we find the answers.

Pat Moon

Contents & Acknowledgements

DEEP IN THE FOREST

Deep in the forest where no-one's ever been
Lives the tiny, flying sprongle that no-one's ever seen.

On the edge of the forest are creatures made of steel,
With jagged teeth and fearsome claws, preparing for the kill;
They've marked out their territory and have the battle planned,
For they feed on the giant trees that guard the sprongle's land.

Deep in the forest, the sprongle doesn't know
That his home is being hunted and there's nowhere else to go.

Deep in the forest, high up in his tree,
Waits the tiny, flying sprongle that we won't ever see.

DANGER SIGN

The notice said

WARNING!

THIS WATER IS POLLUTED

DO NOT FISH OR SWIM

**THE OWNERS ARE NOT RESPONSIBLE
FOR LOSS OF LIFE OR LIMB**

So we gathered up our swimming gear
That we'd no longer need
And wondered should we tell them
That otters cannot read.

FOOD FOR THOUGHT

The man on the television said
That trying to save the world's unfed
Exacerbates the situation
And leads to over-population.
Was he saying, (please discuss),
But only so long as it's them
Not us?

Sing a Song of
CHEMICALS

Sing a song of chemicals
Spraying on the crops,
Killing all the insects
With their lethal drops,
Pumping fertilizers
And nitrates in the earth,
Intensive farmed and blemish-free
We want our money's worth.
The rain is falling from the sky
On to the soil below,
Washing all the chemicals
Into the river's flow,
The fishes in the river
Swim along its bed,
Along come all the chemicals
And kill the fishes dead.

The Elephant

Whoever thought to invent
Such a wondrous beast as the elephant,
With his wrinkly skin and dainty toes,
Protruding teeth and swinging nose?

Whoever wouldn't rather see
An elephant
Than ivory?

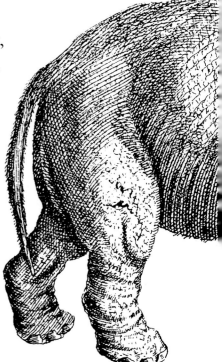

hidermus Indianum

Pachidermus Ino

Finders — Keepers, Losers — Weepers.

Men once found ways to share with Earth,
To give and take in equal worth,
Then passed her on for us to keep.
If we lose her, who'll be here to weep?

13

LITTEROLOGY

When they dig beneath the city
In 2864
And historians look for evidence
Of how men lived before,
Will the life-style and culture
Of twentieth century man
Be represented by the presence
Of the empty ring-pull can?
Will they be enthusiastic
About remains of so much plastic?
Will they carefully be mapping
The position of each wrapping?
Will museums be displaying
Ancient cans once used for spraying
Or building re-constructions
Of hamburger-fry productions,
Or showing the restoring
Of graffiti artists' drawings?
When they dig beneath the city
In 2864
What conclusions will they make about
The men who lived before?

A Cautionary Tale

Little Pete would only eat
Packaged puddings very sweet,
Fizzy drinks with tartrazine,
Pork pies and pastries filled with cream.
He ignored his parents' desperate pleas
To eat vegetables, or fruit or cheese,
For his craving for E2s tabooed
Any sort of healthy food.
Then they noticed with alarm
His legs had started to embalm.
As the process reached his chin,
Still little Pete would not give in,
And to the end his cry was "Never!",
Now little Pete's preserved for ever.
They keep him propped up in the hall
As a warning to you all,
Not to share their young son's fate,
Who perished before his sell-by date.

SEEDS

I never cease to wonder how these seeds,
Each smaller than a full-stop on a page,
Can find in this dull soil, sufficient needs
To metamorphose into seedling stage.

I never understand how this full-stop
Contains so much within its tiny shell;
The leaves that wait to shoot and roots to drop
And phantom flowers, all sealed in a cell.

How in drab seeds and soil even duller,
Can purples, reds and yellows, greens and gold
Be contained, until they spill their colour
Into flowers, like treasure from a hold?

I never cease to wonder year by year,
As I plant new seeds and watch them growing,
And consider as leaves and buds appear
If wonder is improved by the knowing.

TIGER *in a* ZOO

She stalks a steel-branched jungle
And paces concrete grass,
Though her stripes afford poor camouflage
Behind the metal bars.

She paces concrete grass
And sees the horizon shimmer
As beyond the city's drizzle,
The distant mountains glimmer.

She sees the horizon shimmer
Beneath an uncaged sky
And hunts a shadow antelope
As spectral vultures fly.

Beneath an uncaged sky
My imagination stirs.
But the zoo is her world
And has always been;
And the dreams are mine
Not hers.

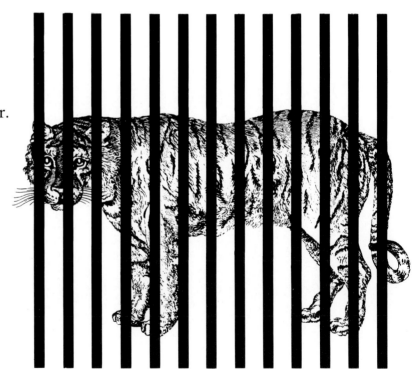

17

With us Always

Here lies Polly Thene.
Her life was very short,
But still her presence lingers
And is never far from thought.
She was used and then discarded,
But now since her release
Remains for all eternity
In an everlasting piece.
Each beach, each field, each wood, each stream
Reminds us of our sorrow
For the body that lies here at rest
Will still be here tomorrow.

I am a
TREE

I am a tree.
Like you
I breathe,
I reproduce.
I too need the warmth of the sun,
The wetness of the rain,
The space to grow.
One difference between us two
Is that
You need me
More than I need you.

Dolphin Mother

I gave birth to him
In the Warm Waters.
Gently I led him upwards
To where the waters meet the air
And he took his first breath.
Already he knew to stay by my side
And how to suckle my milk.
I showed him how to dive and surface
And to make his breath last.
Six full moons later
He began to catch and eat the fish,
To breach and scatter the tuna.
Already he knew how to leap and dive
For the joy of it.
He hunted and played
With the other calves,
Learning the ways of the waters.

Till the day the boat came.

Too late I saw the nets
Which separated me from him
And the others who were caught.
Too late my signals of warning.

How they struggled to break free.
How they lashed the water.
How they tried to force their bodies
Through the nets.
How they gasped for air.
How their eyes pleaded with us.
How we threw ourselves at the nets
And tore at the ropes with our teeth.
How we cried and leapt
As the great nets rose up.
How great was my agony
As I saw my son writhe in his own.
Could the men not see their pain?

Later we found them
Floating on the waters.
We stayed close,
Sheltering them
And urging life
Back into their bodies.
But the breath had gone from them
Forever.
And something inside me
Has also died.

BLUE WHALE

Whale
Who do
You call for?
How many years
Must you seek and wait
Beneath the wide world's waves
Searching solo for a mate?
Did we do right to save
You for such a fate?
Or do you hate
Us, saving
You too
Late?

EATING DISORDER

Please Amanda, just take a taste,
It can't add inches to your waist;
I hate to see food go to waste.

The first year of drought we survived
But the second year two of my children died.

Please Amanda, why do you pick
Your food as if it makes you sick,
When already your arms resemble sticks?

My children now show their bones
And still the soil's as hard as stones.

Please Amanda, why do you hate
Your body in its natural state
And strive to keep it underweight?

I watch my children grow weak and thin
As their bones show sharper under tight skin.

Please Amanda, don't begin a
Row by throwing up your dinner;
How can you possibly want to be thinner?

Today we buried our youngest daughter
Whose bowels ran red from the poisoned water.

Please Amanda, can't you see
That starving yourself is punishing me?

My children, I weep for you;
To watch you die is killing me too.

A Question of Taste

Q.   What's the price of a hamburger please?

A.   Nine square metres of rainforest trees.

Q.   What do you get in a quarter-pounder?

A.   Cow's shin, heart and tongue, some sinew and around a
Quarter's water, colouring, rusk and polyphosphate,
Preservative, chopped fat, monosodium glutamate.

Q.   Well son, what are you waiting for?

A.   I don't think I want it anymore.

The Bird's Nest

My friend and I found a birds' nest
That had fallen from a tree;
Fascinated by its basket-work
We decided to see
If a nest-building contest
Would be won by her or me.
We collected grass and feathers,
Straw and twigs and moss,
And mud for binding
The twigs that lay criss-cross.
Hours later it was evident
That both of us had lost;
For however we plaited the grass,
Threaded, wove or mended,
Our nests resembled bonfire heaps,
So both of us surrendered.
The birds had won; we were outclassed.
We were never real contenders.

How could it be
That a bird's technique
Could beat us and our fingers
Using only its beak?

In the Woods

The squirrel is a show-off
As he scampers up the trees,
Leaping like an acrobat
On the circus high trapeze.

While the badger is so bashful,
He prefers to wear disguise
And never ventures out without
A mask across his eyes.

But the fox is far more streetwise
From his visits to the town,
Where he dines at the finest dustbins
In his suit of rusty brown.

While the owl watches motionless
In contemptuous surprise,
At the hurry and the scurry,
Through round bespectacled eyes.

Night Visitors

Not last night but the night before,
A cross looking tiger came knocking at my door.
I went downstairs to let him in
When I noticed he was wearing another boy's skin.
So I hid until he'd gone away,
Then along came an elephant dressed in grey,
But just in time I saw beneath
She wore a necklace made of human teeth.
I crouched down low so she couldn't see me
When up drove a gorilla in a JCB.
When he started demolishing the garden shed
I'd had enough so I went back to bed.
Come this morning I'm still not sure
Why all those visitors came knocking at my door.

On the beach

Come away from the water Jane,
It's not very clean.
Don't touch the seaweed Jane,
We don't know where it's been.

You can paddle, if you promise Jane
Not to splash about
And to keep your little red wellies on
And wash when you come out.

Come and sit on the blanket Jane,
But be careful where you tread –
There's something nasty in the sand
So play with your doll instead.

It's time for us to go now Jane.
Have you had a nice play?
We'll come and visit the beach again
If you're as good as you were today.

Mustard & Cress

What's that you've brought home?
The mustard and cress I've grown.

Mustard and cress?
Yes.

Have you brought it for me?
No. I'm going to eat it for my tea.

But you hate mustard and cress; you always say it tastes too hot.
That's YOUR mustard and cress; this one's not.

Don't be so silly; there's no difference between the two.
Oh yes there is; this one's much better. This is the one *I* grew.

Broken Promise

Once when I was young
And a little less wise,
I could not wait for the rhododendron bud
To open and tried to prise
The petals into flower.

My eagerness to see
What flower would be presented
By such a promising bud
Was not contented
To wait for the hour.

But the bud was hard and green
And would not unfold.
My nails picked at the layers.
Tore, stripped and holed
The tight skins into a shredded shower.

When I was young
And a little less wise,
I had not learned
To wait for the prize
Of blossom,
Or how greed turns promise sour.

E-types

I like going to Susan's house.
I like going to tea.
They eat food with additives
And things beginning with E.
I had sausages, fried bread and chips,
A can of fizzy drink too,
Followed by strawberry flavoured whip.
What would Mum say if she knew?

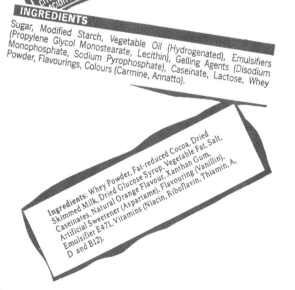

INGREDIENTS
Milk Chocolate (30%), Sugar, Wheatflour,
Animal and Vegetable Fat, Pasteurised Whole
Egg, Dried Glucose Syrup, Glucose Syrup,
Glycerine, Fat-Reduced Cocoa, Emulsifiers:
E471, E475; Soya Flour, Dried Whey, Salt,
Dried Buttermilk, Potassium Caseinate,
Preservative: Potassium Sorbate; Fla...

INGREDIENTS: SUGAR, PLAIN CHOCOLATE,
FLOUR, GLUCOSE SYRUP WHOLE EGG,
CONCENTRATED ORANGE JUICE (8.6% ORANGE
JUICE EQUIVALENT) GELLING AGENT (PECTIN),
VEGETABLE OIL, GLYCERINE, RAISING AGENTS
(SODIUM BICARBONATE, E450a, AMMONIUM
BICARBONATE) NATURAL FLAVOURINGS,
CITRIC ACID, NATURAL COLOUR (TURMERIC),
ACIDITY REGULATOR (SODIUM CITRATE)

INGREDIENTS
Sugar, Modified Starch, Vegetable Oil (Hydrogenated), Emulsifiers
(Propylene Glycol Monostearate, Lecithin), Gelling Agents (Disodium
Monophosphate, Sodium Pyrophosphate), Caseinate, Lactose, Whey
Powder, Flavourings, Colours (Carmine, Annatto).

Ingredients: Whey Powder, Fat-reduced Cocoa, Dried
Skimmed Milk, Dried Glucose Syrup, Vegetable Fat, Salt,
Caseinates, Natural Orange Flavour, Xanthan Gum,
Artificial Sweetener (Aspartame), Flavouring (Vanillin),
Emulsifier E471, Vitamins (Niacin, Riboflavin, Thiamin, A,
D and B12).

MILK CHOCOLATE CONTAINS EMULSIFIER

INGREDIENTS: MILK CHOCOLATE, SUGAR,
PEANUTS, CORNFLOUR, GLUCOSE SYRUP, GUM
ACACIA, COLOURS: E171, E104, E124, E122, E110,
E131, MODIFIED STARCH, GLAZING AGENT:
CARNAUBA WAX

...HIN AND FLAVOURING

Ingredients:
Maize Meal, Vegetable Oil
and Hydrogenated Vegetable
Oil, Starch, Prawn Cocktail
Flavour (Acidity Regulator -
E262; Flavour Enhancer -
621; Citric Acid; Flavouring;
Artificial Sweetener -
Saccharin), Sugar, Salt,
Colours (E110, E160b).

INGREDIENTS: GLUCOSE SYRUP SUGAR, GELATIN,
MODIFIED STARCH, MALIC ACID, ACETIC ACID,
FLAVOURINGS, GLAZING AGENTS: VEGETABLE OIL
AND BEESWAX. COLOURS E122, E104, E127, E142...

INGREDIENTS: Cheddar Cheese, W...
Butter, Emulsifying Salts (E339, E341,
Milk Protein, Salt, Preservative (Potass
Sorbate), Colour (Paprika).

INGREDIENTS:
Dried Potato,
Vegetable Oil,
Starch, Salt,
Emulsifier (E471),
Flavour Enhancer
(621).

...T BEFORE

INGREDIENTS
Whole Milk, Sugar, Cream,
Skim Milk Powder, Cocoa, Glucose,
Soy Protein, Salt,
Stabilisers E407, E410, & E471

If only we'd had another socket there!

At the Flick of a SWITCH

Swish goes the washing machine,
Grrrr goes the grater,
Ping goes the microwave,
Pdpp the percolator,
Brmmmm goes the vacuum cleaner,
Whirrr, the tumble dryer,
Wizzz goes the liquidiser,
Sizzz, the deep-fat fryer.
There goes the thingy-me-bob
That makes the fizzy drinks,
With all the other thingy-me-bobs
To the cupboard under the sink.
Up go more power stations,
Up goes the smoke,
Cough-cough goes this planet,
"You're going to make me choke."

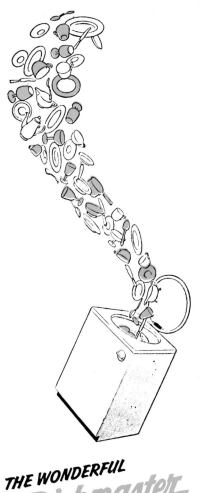

THE WONDERFUL *Dishmaster*

WASHES, RINSES, DRIES—IN ONLY **4** MINUTES

This is the cleaner housewives everywhere are excited about!

NOAH'S ARKS

They must hurry aboard
Before it's too late;
As their homes disappear
There's no time to wait.
For the fields and the forests,
The rivers and trees
Are shrinking and sinking
Beneath human seas.

So in cages, enclosures,
Reservations and parks,
They're taken aboard
The animal arks.
And just like Noah,
They wait inside
To disembark
When the seas subside.

Charlie

"Now this one," said the lady at the cats' home,
"Was found on the tip, in a sealed box, brought in yesterday.
He's small for his age and bites holes in his fur;
You can see he's in a bad way.
We thought perhaps he's about twelve weeks,
But the vet says he's certainly more.
Probably nearer eight or nine months;
It's difficult to be sure."

So we brought him home.
He lay in stiff terror as we
Tried to clean his fur, comb
And cut the tangles free.

He would not be left alone;
Would sleep in fitful naps,
Refusing his bed,
Seeking instead
To settle on warm laps.

Our mealtimes became quite fraught.
He seemed to have no idea
Of how a cat ought
To behave, leaping up
At the table,
Grabbing anything available,
Running off to hide and scoff,
Pouncing again to carry off
His loot of cheese or bread or cake.

So who is this contented cat
Who sits upon the chair,
Watching politely as we eat
With a feigned, disinterested stare?
Who is this handsome cat
With gleaming black fur and white socks?
This is Charlie from the cats' home
Who was left to die in a box.

touch wood

Touch wood and feel her spirit move
in the trembling of her leaves,

Touch wood and smell the perfume
of the precious air she breathes,

Touch wood and taste the flavours
of her fruits that we receive,

Touch wood and see against the sky
the lace her fingers weave,

Touch wood and hear her branches conduct
the rhythm of the breeze,

Touch wood that others take the time
to listen to the trees.

Almost Human

Come and see the people dear.
Oh, look how they sit!
Aren't they sweet
The way they laugh?
I really must admit
That they seem quite intelligent.
Just hear the sounds they make;
You could almost believe
They're trying to communicate.

They're very easily trained
And respond to simple rules.
Just watch how they point and wave
As we swim around the pool.
See how they stand and clap
When we dive through the hoop?
And the noise they make
When we walk on our tails
Or leap the bar in one swoop!

Just watch how they jump and shout
In my favourite part of the shows
When we dive and splash the water
All over the front few rows.

It's time to leave them now, dear,
They've had enough for one day.
It's quite amazing what people can do
If you treat them in the right way.

35

Broken Dream

I dreamed that I could tell the time
By the sun and the stars in the sky,
And my bathroom and kitchen tap
Were the streams that rippled by,
And my larder was the forest
And my music the harmonies
Of bird-song accompanied
By the wood-wind of the trees.
But my mother called me from my sleep
And as I slowly woke
I remembered with a sadness
The beautiful dream that broke.

36

This is the Earth

This is the earth that God made.

These are the seeds
That lay in the earth
That God made.

These are the trees
That grew from the seeds
That lay in the earth
That God made.

These are the men
Who burned the trees,
That grew from the seeds,
That lay in the earth
That God made.

This is the smoke like a shroud which surrounds,
That choked the men
Who burned the trees,
That grew from the seeds,
That lay in the earth
That God made.

This is the air, like a ghost earthbound
That's trapped by the smoke like a shroud which surrounds,
That choked the men
That burned the trees,
That grew from the seeds,
That lay in the earth
That God made.

This is the sun the earth spins round
That warms the air like a ghost earthbound,
That's trapped by the smoke like a shroud which surrounds,
That choked the men
That burned the trees,
That grew from the seeds,
That lay in the earth
That God made.

This is the dust upon the ground,
That's dried by the sun the earth spins round,
That warms the air like a ghost earthbound,
That's trapped by the smoke like a shroud which surrounds,
That choked the men
That burned the trees,
That grew from the seeds,
That lay in the earth
That God made.

This is the rain that flooded and drowned
The dust that lay upon the ground,
That was dried by the sun the earth spins round,
That warms the air like a ghost earthbound,
That's trapped by the smoke like a shroud which surrounds,
That choked the men
That burned the trees,
That grew from the seeds,
That lay in the earth
That God made.

No man, no beast, no tree, no sound
Disturb the waters that flooded and drowned
The dust that lay upon the ground,
That was dried by the sun the earth spins round,
That warms the air like a ghost earthbound,
That's trapped by the smoke like a shroud which surrounds,
That choked the men
That burned the trees,
That grew from the seeds,
That lay in the earth
That God made.

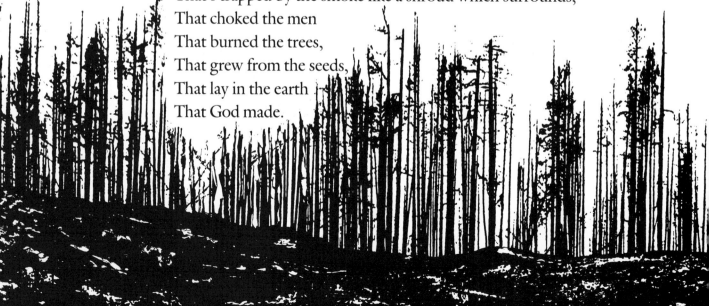

Earth's
CLOCK

Imagine that the earth was shaped
Twenty four hours ago,
Then at 6 a.m. rains fell from the skies
To form the seas below.
At 8 a.m. in these soupy seas
The first signs of life appeared.
The dinosaurs called seventy minutes ago
But at twenty to twelve disappeared.
Man arrived just one minute ago
Then at thirty seconds to midnight,
Raised himself from his stooping stance
And started walking upright.
In the thirty seconds man's walked the earth
See what he's managed to do.

Earth's clock continues ticking;
The rest is up to you.

·RHINOCEROS·

It's preposterous
That rhinoceros
Has to keep on his toes,
But the fact is
It's hazardous
For him to show
His nose,
For though he isn't venomous,
(He doesn't sting or bite),
There's someone trying to get at
This thunderous delight.
So he's not at all gregarious,
In fact he's quite withdrawn
With the worry
That somebody
Is going to steal
His horn.

Beauty Free

Her lips are glistening;
Mine are inflamed.
Her eyes are sparkling;
Mine are maimed.
Her skin glows gently;
Mine is raw.
Her hair shines softly;
My fur is no more.
Her beauty's displayed;
I'm hidden away.
The sight of me
Would be too much to pay.

My Pal Al

My pal Al
Plays around in school,
But let me tell you something,
He's nobody's fool.

My pal Al
Never seems to worry;
Just smiles that slow smile of his,
He's never in a hurry.

My pal Al
Can mend a broken bike,
Take it apart, put it back,
Anything you like.

My pal Al
Keeps pigeons in a shed;
Built it all by himself;
Designed it in his head.

My pal Al
Knows where the herons nest,
Where the badgers feed
And where the fishing's best.

My pal Al
Is nobody's fool.
He knows all sorts of things
They don't teach you in school.

Litter Free (at last!)

There was a young man from Kent
Who dropped litter wherever he went.
It made his wife cry
For their home was a sty,
And the piles had begun to ferment.

One day, quite carelessly,
He fell in and couldn't break free;
In the litter he died,
While his grieving wife cried,
"It was suicide –
Litterally."

EARTH, SEA & MOON

"Why is it men have named their world
After you?" demanded Sea,
"When you're weak and small and powerless
And there's so much more of me."

"I'm dependable," said Earth,
"Men trust me while they sleep,
Whilst you're so unpredictable;
Sometimes shallow, sometimes deep."

"But I offer them adventure
And new countries to explore,
And give them food to eat," cried Sea;
"It's me they should adore!"

"You're so moody," Earth continued,
"Sometimes gentle like a kitten,
Then raging like a tiger
That's been very badly bitten.
Whilst I'm more reliable
In everything I do.
It's natural men should worship me
And never trust in you."

46

"We'll see who's master of this world!"
Bellowed the furious Sea,
"I'll swallow you in just one bite,
Then men will worship me."

Sea's muscles greenly rippled
As he reared to his fullest height;
He roared to show his spittle-flecked mouth
Then lunged and took a bite.

As Sea's wet mouth devoured her,
Earth called with dying breath
For her sister Moon to save her
From her cold and watery death.

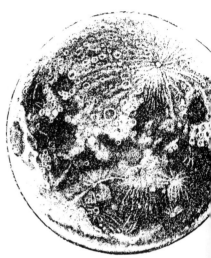

Moon heard her cries and stretched to reach
Sea's slippery tail in her hand
And pulled and pulled and pulled till Earth
Was safely back on land.

And twice daily ever since that time
Sea keeps creeping up and sighing
As he fails again to swallow Earth;
But still he goes on trying.

While high above floats Sister Moon
Who promised always to follow
Her sister Earth, and grab Sea's tail
Each time he tries to swallow.

A MESSAGE
FROM A LONG SERVING MEMBER
OF THE BROWN PARTY

Vote for me
Your friendly earthworm,
Conservationist
Born and bred.
When I take your soil
I'll always give
Something better back instead.
I'm into things organic
And really most concerned
That you cast your vote
To ensure
The earthworm
Is returned.

COVER STORY

The orange's waxy rind unwinds,
Banana skin's easily shedable,
The cob-nut comes in a crackable case,
And the apple's skin is edible.
The egg is delivered exquisitely wrapped,
Its shell the perfect packet;
Oh would this plastic-sealed Cheddar cheese
So easily shed its jacket.

AIR RAID

Like giant cannons aiming high,
The chimneys fire their ammunition
At the sky.

On the ground, regiments of traffic mass
To launch assaults
Of poisoned gas.

Like survivors of a holocaust, shorn and bare,
Skeletal trees point bony fingers,
Accusing the air.

The mountain, stripped, exposes naked sides
To barrages of wind and rain.
Rocks fall; mud slides.

Bombardments of bitter rain drift down
Into the lake
And fishes drown.

Whilst high above, as if in pain,
Battle-scarred stone saints weep wounding tears
Of acid rain.

Prophecy

I am where life began;
I saw the fish first crawl,
I carried you to unknown worlds,
I pillowed Icarus's fall.

I am the cradle of legend
Where monsters lie in wait,
Where serpents dwell and Neptune rules
His watery estate.

Within my depths, a kingdom
Of creatures great and small,
Of cold, dark worlds you'll never see,
Where canyons rise and fall.

I am genesis
On which all life depends,
For as I signalled life's beginning
So shall I sign life's end.

For when fishes drown
And the whale has gone,
And birds no longer fly,
Then my blood will thicken
And the life within shall die.

DYING QUIETLY

These children die quietly;
No headlines screaming across the page,
No rage from politicians blaming others,
No mothers appearing on our screens,
Seen waving banners asking why
Did her child and forty thousand others die
Today.
The way they die is quietly.
Not for the want of a miracle cure;
Pure water, food, simple medications are all they're needing.
So proceedings will not be taken out;
Without a voice
No choice but to die
Unheard.
The words must come
From others.

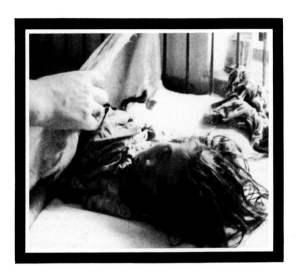

"Some fifteen million small children die each year . . . They die very quietly; one hears very little about them; they come from the world's poorest families, who themselves are the weakest and the most powerless members of those powerless families."

James Grant, UNICEF

The Ostrich

Whenever the ostrich was worried
In the sand she buried her head.
She did it when the wolf came by
And now her chicks are dead.

Later when the lion came by
She buried her head as before;
It lies severed beneath the sand now
But she's not worried any more.

SONG
of the
HEDGEHOG

Praise be for creepy-crawlies
And slimy, slippery things,
With their crunchy parts and juices
That every new night brings.

Praise be for rambling gardens
And the warm compost heap,
For unswept leaves and hedges
That offer peaceful sleep.

Praise be for all earth's wonders;
For dry, secluded ditches,
For tasty frogs and lizards
And for my bristly breeches.

Praise be for sleep in winter
And safekeeping till I wake,
But praise be most of all
For cars that swerve or brake.

Today's TOMORROW

Today the seed –
Tomorrow the grain.
Today the planting –
Tomorrow the gain.

Today's now –
Tomorrow's then.
Today's children –
Tomorrow's men.

Tonight's darkness –
Tomorrow's light.
Tonight's blindness –
Tomorrow's sight.

Today's sword –
Tomorrow's plough.
Today's decisions –
Tomorrow's now.

She pulled the tab that says *TEAR HERE*
But alas, the tab tore clear.
She tried to peel the sealed end-flaps
But nothing could prise back those wraps.
What could she do to extract
Those biscuits so inscrutably wrapped?
She took a knife and attacked it,
Sawed and slashed, stabbed and hacked it.
Really thought that she had cracked it
Till she surveyed the stubborn packet.
From the wraps so tightly sealed
At last the biscuits were revealed,
But her plan had not succeeded,
"Oh crumbs," she said,
"That's all I needed."

Riddle

We don't plan
Our future,
We travel
On the breeze,
We adapt
To all conditions
And live
Just where
We please.
We push up
Through the concrete
Where nothing else
Could thrive,
We're tenacious
And resilient
In our struggle
To survive.
You attack us,
You uproot us,
You treat us
With disdain,
Then when you think
We're beaten,
We spring right up again.

We smile at you
From roadsides,
We add colour
To your walls,
We offer food
And shelter
Despite your
Urban sprawls.
Our virtues
Lie undiscovered
Like our tiny,
Buried seeds.
Can you guess
Who we are?
We are

The weeds

58

To Make a Fur Hat

Take one gun,
Take one leopard
And shoot it in the head;
(Aim so as not to damage the pelt),
Then make quite sure it's dead.
Slit belly with a very sharp knife,
Tugging gently as it cuts,
Pulling the skin away from the flesh;
Discard the carcase and guts.
Stretch the skin,
Then allow it to dry;
Clean fur while it's still stretched flat.
This should be sufficient
To make an attractive hat.

N.B.
If hat is successful
And matching coat is desired,
Repeat as above forty times or more
According to size required.

Antarctic Kingdom

At the end of the world is a kingdom
Where crystal castles stand;
Where solitary icy sentinels
Guard its fragile land.

At the end of the world is a kingdom
Where frozen fortresses float;
Where silver serpents with teeth of ice
Ride its glacial moat.

At the end of the world is a kingdom
With palaces of white,
Within which dwell its King of Ice
And his consort Queen of Light.

At the end of the world is a kingdom
Where winter never dies
And the King and the Queen harness the wind
And ride the storms in the skies.

At the end of the world is a kingdom
Where the wind sings all year long,
And the King and Queen dance in marbled halls
To its shrilling, soaring song.

At the end of the world live a king and queen
Whose guardians defend
Their fragile, crystal kingdom
That can break but never mend.

For the world will end in this kingdom
Should its guardians ever falter,
And the Queen of Light will fade away
And the King will turn to water

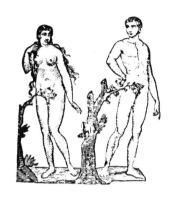

Men of Clay

If Adam was shaped from earth's rough clay
What creature would God make
From the poisoned and eroded soil
That we've left in our wake?

Cat Day

This is a cat day;
A day for purring in the sun,
Not stirring to finish
All the work that waits undone.

This is a cat day;
A day to be enjoyed,
Not employed in fetching,
But stretching in the sun.

This is a cat day;
A day for watching
Through half-closed eyes
The shadows creep across the grass
And the fluttering butterflies.

This is a cat day;
To pounce upon,
To snatch,
For capturing alive;
This is a day to catch.